I0214108

My Publishing Journey

A GIFT FROM

. . . .

THIS BOOK BELONGS TO

. . . .

THIS BOOK CHRONICLES THE JOURNEY OF (BOOK'S TITLE)

. . . .

*Praise and glory to our Lord and Savior Jesus Christ
who built this company and created the talent within.
May we serve you with joy all of our lives.*

*Our deepest gratitude to all who contributed to this book.
Without you, we'd still be dreaming.*

© 2016 Tamara Dever and Erin Stark

All rights reserved. No part of this book may be reproduced in any form or by any electronic
or mechanical means, including information storage and retrieval systems, without permission
in writing from the publisher, except by a reviewer who may quote brief passages in a review.

TLC GRAPHICS, *TLCGraphics.com* and *MyBookJourney.com*

Book design © TLC Graphics, *TLCGraphics.com;*
Cover and interior illustrations © Elizabeth Dotterer, *ElizabethDottererArt.com*

Stock art: Patterned papers from Seventh Avenue Designs; Art on pages 44, 52, 54, 62 from DepositPhotos.com; Art on
pages 12, 28, 30, 36, 42, 43, 45, 46, 47, 60 from GraphicStock.com; Metal pins from Marcee Duggar Designs via Deal Jumbo

ISBN: 978-0-692-68392-7

Contents

WITH THE
POSSIBLE EXCEPTION
OF THE EQUATOR,
EVERYTHING BEGINS
SOMEWHERE.

C. S. LEWIS

Introduction

CONGRATULATIONS! Whether you're just getting started or are already holding that new book in your hands, this is a wonderful accomplishment. As a published author, you're going to make a difference in the lives of your readers. Whether you have a cause, are sharing information, or aim to entertain, your book is poised to influence someone out there to do something new or think in a different way.

Publishing a book is truly a journey — often into the unknown — full of thrills, doubts, details, and excitement. The details that make up this amazing adventure are what make publishing each book so unique. *My Publishing Journey* is not aimed at showing you how to write, publish, or sell your book. There are plenty of reference materials and professionals to help with that. This guided journal is a place to document each moment that makes your publishing journey so special.

Blessings and bon voyage!

Jami   *Erin*   *Monica*

TAMARA DEVER, ERIN STARK, and MONICA THOMAS
TLC Graphics

Six-Month Book Production Timeline

WHAT TO DO AFTER YOUR MANUSCRIPT IS COMPLETE

MONTH 1	MONTH 2	MONTH 3	MONTH 4
EDITING			
FRONT COVER DESIGN			*Note: Editing happens before design begins and proofreading happens after.*
Complete illustrations, if using, prior to design.	**INTERIOR DESIGN AND LAYOUT**		
	BACK COVER AND SPINE DESIGN		
		PROOFREAD	
MARKETING AND PR PLANNING	Develop author website, blog, social media pages to build your all-important platform	Plan author tour (live and online), set advertising schedule	Send review copies, announce to trade
Here are things you can do to promote your book while it's in production.		**PRINT ADVANCE READER COPIES**	**INDEXING**
		Also called ARCs	**MAKE FINAL CHANGES**

NOTES ABOUT YOUR OWN TIMELINE:

his is an example of the order and timing
or a typical book's production schedule.
ctual times will vary, as each project is unique.

MONTH 5	MONTH 6

You're published! Keep on marketing!

BOOK RELEASE DATE

Send press releases, pitch for interviews, work social media, finalize launch party

E-BOOK CONVERSION

FINAL PRINTING

Before Writing

Before that first word was ever written, there was a purpose for it. Somebody needs to hear what you have to say. That blank page is an opportunity, so make a mark on it — any mark — and move forward!

During a decade as editor-in-chief at a medium-sized publishing house, it was my displeasure to write rejection letters. Many of those rejection letters could have been acceptance letters had the authors spent additional time planning before they began writing. Here are five suggestions to help make your publishing journey a pleasant and successful one:

- *Survey the competition.* Are you the first to write about this topic? If not, what will you offer to make your book unique?

- *Survey your readers.* Who are your customers? Find a few of them and tell them your ideas. Learn from their reactions.

- *Envision the book.* Find a book that looks about as you imagine yours. Count the words on a typical page and multiply that by the total number of pages. That will tell you roughly how many words you'll need for your book.

- *Be aware of the standard framework.* All books include title page, table of contents, dedication, etc. These are your responsibility, too. Don't be surprised on deadline day by a blank page where your preface was supposed to be.

- *Write a detailed outline.* Do not just begin typing! Would you start a cross-country trip without looking at a map (or your GPS)? Know precisely where you're going and how you're going to get there.

What you write and how you write it will be key to your book's success. But knowing exactly where you're headed and how you'll get there will make your trip pleasant and fulfilling.

May your literary journey be delightful from start to finish!

DICK CHRISTIANSON, editor, author, and
– most important – book lover!

What prompted you to write this book?

....

....

....

Date you decided to write it: ....

Is this your first book? If not, what else have you written? Published?

....

....

....

How did others react when you told them you were going to write a book?

....

....

....

....

Who supported you?

....

....

....

....

....

Describe your book in two sentences. (This is your "elevator pitch.")

....

....

....

....

....

....

Who is your book's intended audience? (Age range, professional status, interest group)

....

....

....

....

What does being a successful author mean to you? How do you define success?

....

....

....

....

....

....

....

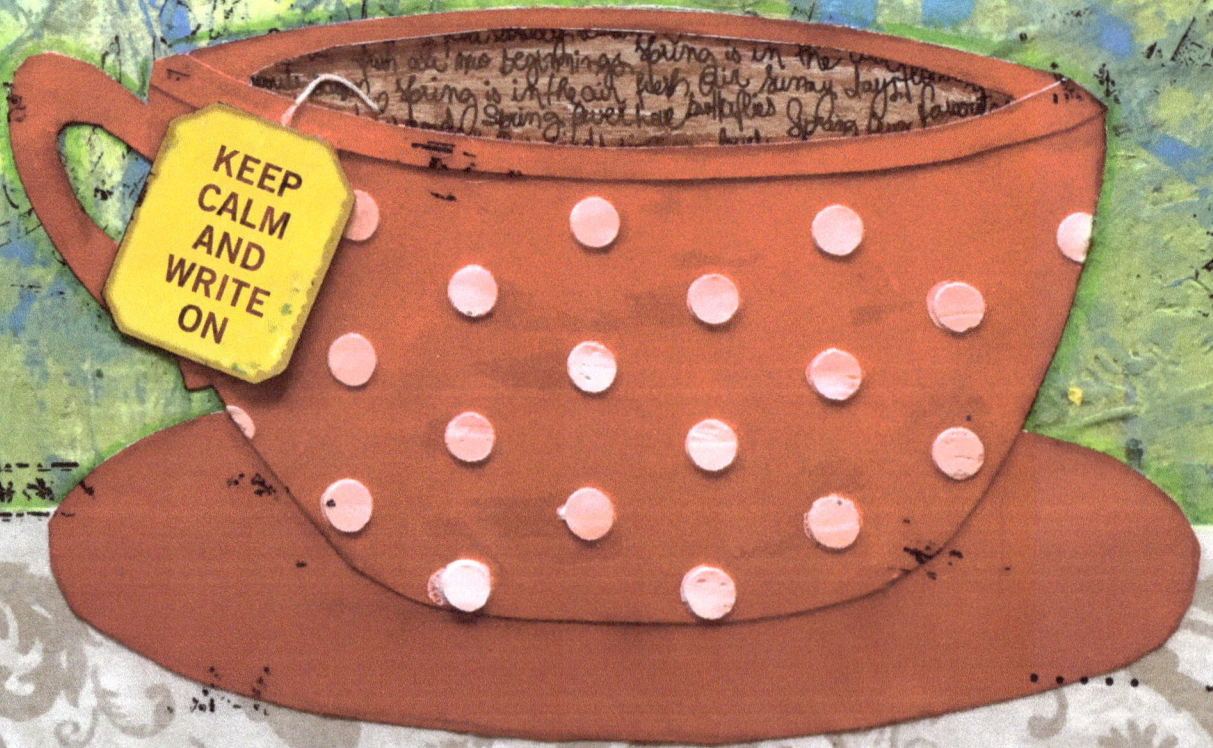

KEEP
CALM
AND
WRITE
ON

patience

While Writing

"Why would someone want to read my book?" Authors struggle with this thought every day. The way to overcome this doubt is to keep your focus in the right place — your reader. Write your message in your voice, but never forget that the book you're pouring your heart and soul into is ultimately for a reader who needs that message. Without the reader, your writing is simply an exercise.

I wrote my first book three times. In 2000 I wanted to write a book as part of my ministry. I wouldn't show that first draft to anyone. It was aimless and all about me — what *I* wanted to spill on the page instead of what would benefit the reader. I also needed to find my voice.

Four years later, after having articles published, finding my voice, and learning that writing is about the reader, I took another shot at the book. While the writing was better and I had an outline that made sense, I knew it still wasn't right. Several missing pieces and some rough edges needed to be resolved.

In 2006 I scrapped most of the material in my second draft and rewrote the book again. This time everything came together; the content was geared for the reader, the writing was sharp, and the outline was sound. Most importantly, I had learned that I needed to soak the writing process in prayer, a discipline I still maintain today.

MIKE GENUNG, author, *The Road to Grace*
RoadtoGrace.net

LAVENDER AND LAUNDRY

A Humble Writing Tip from the French Countryside

Whether a beginner or a multi-published author, there is one thing all writers struggle with: the very next word. I used to think that after years of practice, this what-to-say-next crisis would just go away — as would all my awkward first-essays — but it doesn't (and those essays are forever in cyberspace, where I keep them as a gentle measure of progress).

Some time ago I learned a few tricks to get those elusive words to spill out, and I am going to share these with you here. Ready? Now grab some wet laundry and follow me outside! More than a fresh perspective, the under-rated clothesline offers a host of help when our creative thoughts become stale.

Walking down to the laundry line, a heavy basket on my hip, the fresh scent of rosemary produces a heady effect (heady! That's what we're going for, a little spin of the gray matter to get those words perc-o-lating again!). A row of lavender is also planted beneath my clothesline so that the linens will brush against the flower's fragrant leaves in the breeze. And there is another sneaky reason for lining my

Now grab some wet laundry & follow me outside!

garden with aromatic herbs: like the rosemary (good for memory) the lavender is relaxing (good for bringing forth new ideas). These herbal scents are like smelling salts, reviving our halted creativity!

By the time I begin to hang my family's laundry I am already chattering to myself, evidence that my brain has gone to work trying out new blocks of words. As I continue to pin up socks and T-shirts, I notice a further benefit for the stalled writer: the repetitive, mechanical movement of bending and reaching for laundry causes my brain to begin to shift ... until those words I had grasped for earlier are suddenly near! Forming themselves into sentences! It is time to grab them and run right back to my computer to spill out the rest of the paragraph!

Voilà, a simple but effective tip from my writing perch here in the countryside. But don't sweat it if you don't have a laundry line or lavender — a stroll to the mailbox is enough to get the writing engine going again. Just keep moving. And bring smelling salts along if necessary!

Kristin Espinasse, writer of French-Word-a-Day.com, author, *Words in a French Life, Blossoming in Provence,* and *First French Essais*

What is the first line you wrote? Did it make it into the final version?

....

....

....

Date you wrote that first line: ....

What program and computer did you use?

....

How long did it take for you to write the book? ....

Where do you get your inspiration?

....

....

....

....

What did you do to get past writer's block?

....

....

....

....

....

....

Negative thoughts and how you combated against them:

....

....

....

....

....

....

Significant happenings while writing:

....

....

....

....

....

....

....

....

....

....

....

....

KEEP
CALM
AND
WRITE
ON

YOU

ARE

NOT

IN

THIS

ALONE

Building Your Team

Self-publishing doesn't necessarily mean doing every piece of it yourself. Like any successful business, it means putting together a great team and trusting each member to do his or her job well. The quality of your book's production can make or break its success. Hire professionals to round out your team and spend your valuable time doing what you do best.

. . . .

When you decide to write and publish a book, you are embarking on an exciting journey. Whether you plan to seek traditional channels or self-publish, ensure that your trip is successful by connecting with published authors and established groups right away.

Writing may be a passion, but publishing is a business. Working in isolation can make you an easy mark for unscrupulous companies passing themselves off as legitimate publishers with the intent of overcharging and misleading you. Instead, connect with professionals who can offer you time-saving and sure-footed publishing advice. While critique groups can be helpful, I suggest you also join groups dedicated to the business of publishing such as The Alliance of Independent Authors, Independent Book Publishers Association, National Association of Memoir Writers, She Writes, and Society of Children's Book Writers and Illustrators. Consult *Publishers Weekly* online to discover current local and international conferences and fairs where you can meet other authors, publishing professionals, and vendors. Through groups like these you'll benefit from resources, advice, and tips that it would take years to discover on your own, and you'll learn from authors who are already successful.

FLORA MORRIS BROWN, Ph.D., author and publishing coach,
Color Your Life Happy: Create Your Unique Path and Claim the Joy You Deserve, 2nd ed.

IT TAKES A VILLAGE
Gathering Your Team

When you embark on true self-publishing, you create a publishing company. That isn't as hard as it sounds and often is as simple as filing a DBA under an existing company. In choosing this route, you become a publisher and take on all the responsibilities filled by a traditional publisher. It is important to produce a high-quality book that meets the standards of a traditional publisher if you want your book to be viable in the marketplace. To do this you must assemble a team that replicates the roles of a publishing company. These roles include:

- **PUBLISHING CONSULTANT OR BOOK SHEPHERD** This specialist is experienced in publishing and can ensure you are doing all the necessary things to produce a high quality book. They can help manage the timeline and budget and coordinate the services of the rest of the team.

- **EDITOR** You will need copyediting at a minimum and may also need developmental or substantive editing. This should be someone who is professionally trained as a book editor — not just someone who has a degree in English.

- **BOOK DESIGNER** Choose a designer with specific experience in creating and producing books. Their role will include cover design, interior design, and layout. This could be more than one person but is often a group of services done by an individual.

- **INDEXER** This person has specific training and uses specialized software to develop a professional index for non-fiction books.

- **EBOOK CONVERTER** This person converts your print book to both EPUB and mobi file formats so it can be read on Kindle and other eReaders.

- **PRINTER** How will you produce copies of your book? Options include print on demand (POD), digital, or offset printing.

- **WEBSITE DEVELOPER** He or she assists you in creating a new website for your book and your work as an author. They may work to add information about your book to your existing business website.

- **MARKETING SUPPORT** This person or company can help develop the marketing plan and then implement the marketing strategies.

- **PUBLICIST** A book publicist will help you get media exposure and coverage for you and your book.

- **VIRTUAL ASSISTANT** This person can lend support throughout the process of writing and publishing your book and continued marketing. Believe it or not, there are people who are certified as Professional Virtual Author Assistants.

Where can you find your team? Ask friends who have published books for recommendations, seek out people through local freelancer organizations, check the acknowledgment pages and copyright pages of other books. Ask your other team members; they are often some of the best sources since they have often worked on projects with people who provide services in the role you are seeking.

Janica Smith, Chief Publishing Navigator, PublishingSmith
PublishingSmith.com

Did you hire a book shepherd, mentor, or planner to guide you through the process? (Name, company, contact info, date hired)

....

....

....

....

Did you try to find an agent?

....

....

....

What made you choose to self-publish?

....

....

....

....

If you're publishing, you're starting a company. What is your company's name? What is the significance of the name you chose?

....

....

....

....

....

....

....

Place the logo here, if you have one.

How did you finance the project? What costs were involved?

....

....

....

....

How did you feel when you signed your first contract to begin the publishing process?

....

....

....

....

....

What is your book's ISBN? ....

Editorial

A good editor is an author's best friend, massaging and finessing your work to enhance your message without changing your voice. Working with a quality and experienced book editor is a critical first step in moving toward producing a great final product.

. . . .

Leaning on a good editor in the writing process is crucial for you sharing your story with the world. The value of a good editor and your relationship with that editor is key in your journey as an author. As a first-time writer, I had great hesitation and doubt that I had to fight through to complete my project. Two of my greatest concerns were whether my grammar and sentence structure would be good enough, and if people would even read my book. Fortunately, I found an amazing editor whose work ethic was impeccable. She was extremely thorough and knowledgeable and from the first time she looked at my work, I was confident in her ability. My book was in the very best hands possible, and she would not only help me, but also enhance my finished product. She challenged me to dig deeper, yet assured me that I was capable and on the right path. Since I had never been through the process before, I was unaware of what to expect. However, my editor was extremely good at communicating every step to me and helping me navigate the do's and don'ts. Since my editor was extremely thorough, I was free to be creative without the pressure of being perfect. I knew my editor would research my content, diligently correct my mistakes, and unapologetically tell me when I was wrong. Through the process of writing and rewriting, leaning on a good editor allowed me to concentrate on my creativity, leaving the structure and correction process in her hands. Finding an editor you can fully trust is not only beneficial, but also essential in creating a rich experience as an author.

KELLY MASTER, speaker, advocate, author of *Shine*
KellyMaster.com

NAME, COMPANY, CONTACT INFO, DATE YOU HIRED EACH EDITING PROFESSIONAL

Editor: . . . .

. . . .

. . . .

Proofreader: . . . .

. . . .

. . . .

Indexer: . . . .

. . . .

. . . .

Ghostwriter: . . . .

. . . .

. . . .

A WORD ABOUT EDITING…

Congratulations! Becoming an author is a very brave endeavor and very rewarding…if some guidelines are followed. A great idea, a super cover, a design that will knock their socks off, and a place to market your self-published book…that's all you need, right? Not so fast….

Have you ever read a book that held your interest for the first half and then started falling apart?

Or how about a book that promised so much — for example, "Help is here for that lawn!" or "This is the best book on traveling in Costa Rica ever!"— yet it fails to keep its promise? Was it because the author didn't really know what she was talking about — or perhaps she failed to hire an editor who could help ensure that promise was fulfilled?

A professional book editor, unlike your next-door neighbor who used to be a teacher or "reads a lot," is going to read your manuscript with a critical eye and tell you where and how you are missing the mark. That's her job!

An editor will point out where and how your book fails to keep its promise. She or he will find the pesky little glitches that can be ruinous to a potentially great book. Misspelled words, poor grammar, confusing headings, sentences that run on and on, and careless writing that

Find an editor you trust and will be a partner in this journey.

doesn't hold a reader's attention are all fair game for an editor's attention.

Your book will likely need the assistance of both a developmental editor and a copy editor. A developmental editor (sometimes called a content editor) should be called in early to help. She will ask, What is your goal for this book? and Who is your intended audience? These are two huge decisions on your part and the developmental editor can help you decide on and achieve those goals. She also will ensure your voice is maintained throughout your book. The copy editor, on the other hand, will be more concerned with the nuts and bolts, polishing the nearly completed content so it shines.

Of course, there is a lot more to an editor's job, but your main job is to find an editor you trust and can talk to, who will be a trusted partner in this journey. She or he will be candid about procedures and costs, and available for questions or feedback along the way. She also should have expertise in your genre as well as credentials and good references. You may never meet your editor (she may be in California, you in New Jersey) but that won't matter. Email, phone and Skype work just fine for this important task in getting your great idea for a book into print!

Barbara Munson, Munson Communications Editorial Services
MunsonCommunications.com

How did you feel about someone else tweaking your writing?

....

....

....

....

....

....

Describe the overall editorial process.

....

....

....

....

....

....

PRETTY

WITH

A

PURPOSE

Design & Illustration

Design and illustration go far beyond aesthetics. Both are a means of conveying information and a way to get the attention of your book's buyers and readers. When used properly, they not only reflect, but elevate your message.

When I began digital illustrating in 2011, I jumped into Photoshop. My son and I wrote a story together, but I flew solo to illustrate. I had no formal training, yet no matter how much I blundered the results seemed magical.

Every page of my first children's book took hundreds of hours. I created layouts in Photoshop and printed several soft cover copies that I took to the Independent Book Publishers Association's annual Publishing University that year. I was eager to meet with publishing professionals for advice and believed the book was ready for press with small tweaks. Their feedback surprised me.

Each expert found the illustrations appealing, but pointed out a major flaw. The book lacked graphic design that integrates the story and illustrations. As a novice illustrator, I had focused on individual images, unaware of an overall design concept. I understand now that it's a common mistake, but I had no idea how to fix it.

By chance, the workshop after my last meeting was all about book design. It emphasized the importance of effective layouts that help the eye flow across a page and through a book. I learned the difference between illustration that depicts a story and graphic design that places and scales visual elements for best visual impact. In short, I needed a book designer.

Soon after, I hired the workshop instructors to redesign the book. I couldn't be happier because their revisions helped earn top reviews and five national awards. For my second book, I didn't hesitate to work with them again. Again, the results are stellar reviews and two top awards, including a children's book of the year nomination — so far.

JO ANN KAIRYS, author, *Sunbelievable* and *I Want Cake!*
StoryQuestBooks.com

HOW DO I FIND THE RIGHT DESIGN PROFESSIONAL?

A book's cover and interior design have great influence on whether reviewers and buyers investigate a title further. Design goes beyond aesthetics and is a means of conveying information and getting the attention of buyers.

Because design is so important, work with an experienced designer specializing in books. While most graphic designers could help you with at least some aspects of creating a book, one who specializes in books can guide you through the whole process and provide the experience and knowledge that can help you avoid hassles and save both time and money. Note that some designers do only covers or interiors, while others are talented at both.

How do you find the right designer to add to your team?

- Ask other publishers and authors whose designs you admire.

- Look at many samples of a designer's work. Does your book fit in their portfolio? Most designers have a range of styles, but nobody can do it all.

- Talk to the designer and listen to your gut feeling. If you don't click, don't hire them!

- Talk with their other clients. Ask: Was your deadline ever in jeopardy because of the designer? Why? How was the problem remedied? How many front cover designs were you given? If you provided any initial ideas, were they built upon or discarded completely? (A good designer will do at least one layout using your idea and others with her own.)

- Ask how many years of experience she has and how many books she has designed.

- Does he know the elements of a typical book cover? How about the interior?

- Ask how designing a hardcover is different from a paperback and if there's a difference in cost.

- Can the designer handle getting the files to pre-press properly? Ask to speak with printers that have worked with the designer.

- Designers are not usually illustrators. Illustrators draw or paint custom pictures. Designers pull together the elements of a page (illustrations or photographs, text, colors, etc.) to create an overall design that is visually pleasing and saleable.

- Sign a written contract covering exactly what will be produced, the timeline, and the cost. Unless the contract states that ownership is being transferred, the designer will automatically own the design. Expect your designer to keep unlimited rights to use images of your book for their promotional purposes.

- It's tempting to spend a few hundred dollars for a cover or interior, but don't! It's terrible to learn that nobody will distribute, promote, or buy your book because it hasn't been properly produced. You end up spending more time and money to do it right the second time. It's worth every penny when you choose to work with a reputable firm.

In all, you'll get better sales results and the respect you deserve with high-quality cover and interior designs and great end-product becomes a sure thing when you hire a carefully-selected, experienced book designer who has your best interest at heart.

Did you hire a cover designer? (Name, company, contact info, date hired)

....

....

Did you hire a designer for the interior? (Name, company, contact info, date hired)

....

....

....

How did you react to seeing your first set of book covers?

....

....

....

Was it difficult to choose a cover? ....

Place your initial front cover designs and/or final front cover here.

How did you react to seeing your book's interior design?

....

....

....

....

How was the overall design process?

....

....

....

....

....

....

Did you hire an illustrator? (Name, company, contact info, date hired)

....

....

....

How did you feel when you first saw your characters come to life?

....

....

....

....

....

....

....

....

....

Paste initial sketches here.

Printing

You're nearly there! Are you finding it difficult to let your baby go? That's normal. You're probably nervous and excited at the same time. Take a deep breath and trust that you and your team have done your very best. Soon, you'll see your final book and feel the joy of having accomplished something big!

The ups, the downs, the last minute changes, the frantic questions begin again. *Did I miss anything? Is it really complete?* Take a deep breath. Sign the approval to go to press. *But what if...? Should I look over it one more time?* No, it is finished. Scan and send the approval. Breathe....

This was the day my book went to the printer, the day we all strive to reach. It was finally here. Peace, but for only a moment. Only then did the realization that this PDF file that only a handful of people had seen was really going be a book, a Bible study that people would read. At this point, all I could do was pray — for the people at the printing company, for the ladies who designed it, for God to open the doors for this Bible study to reach the people He intended it to reach.

Finally, the day arrived for the books to be delivered. As the truck pulled into the parking lot, my heart felt like it would explode. The delivery driver couldn't help but notice my excitement and asked what was in the boxes. I told him it was a Bible study that I had the honor of penning and publishing. He then shared that his teenaged granddaughter had just been baptized. The Lord led me to give him the first book off the truck as a gift to her. Not expecting much of a reaction, I handed him the book. With tears in his eyes, he asked if he could hug me and said it was the best tip he had ever received. In that moment, any fear or doubt I had during and about this process melted away. God allowed me to see what He had in store for this Bible study He had written on my heart.

BRENNA MARSHALL, author, *From the Ground Up*
TBMarshallMinistry.com

GETTING YOUR BOOK INTO BUYERS' HANDS PROFITABLY

By now I'm sure you realize that publishing is a business, and it is a business with a lot of moving parts. While it is one of the easiest businesses to enter today, there are still a lot of considerations that can help you toward success — whatever "success" means for you and your book. Publishing is finance, product development, manufacturing, operations, marketing and PR, and management.

Many of your financial decisions involve the actual product itself (design and printing, programming for ebooks, ancillary products), but many short- and long-term decisions involve life-cycle marketing and product distribution.

- How are you going to get that book into the hands of the buyer once you have convinced them to buy it?

- Will you sell in the back of the room after speeches or in classrooms?

- Do you want to be available in bookstores and other retail stores?

- Do you have a solid platform and sales channel of your own?

- Is your book a good candidate for bulk sales to corporations or associations?

- Are you publishing a legacy piece for your company?

Make your decisions on printing and distribution from realistic and thoughtful evaluation of things like sales potential, returns, discounts, storage and fulfillment, ROI, and your willingness (and ability) to sustain the product with money, time, and energy. These decisions must be made outside of your love for the words you have woven together. I know it's your baby, but don't allow emotion to get in the way of solid planning and execution.

Remember, whenever you print books, you will have to store them in a climate-controlled environment (which you may have to pay for), insure them, inventory them, package and ship them, and even make sure they aren't absorbing odors (like smoke, industrial, or food from nearby items being stored).

Order only as many as you think you will need in a six-month period. Knowing how many you can sell, how you will fulfill those orders, your discount structures for wholesalers and retailers, and your cost of goods sold will be crucial to your success as a publisher.

Keep in mind that printers and manufacturers exist to sell printing and manufacturing. Ask yourself why printers don't ask how the book is being sold and fulfilled when you are ordering printing. Just because your unit cost goes lower when you order more doesn't mean you should do it. Do the math on the other factors involved with ordering a print run of any significant quantity.

What's the takeaway? Always figure the bottom line and know all of the calculations for your distribution channels. Would print-on-demand help you deliver your product on budget and with little hassle? Do you need a print run to reach your audience with the product they want?

Finally, there has never been a better time to publish because there are so many ways to find consumers. When you think of your book as a solution to a problem rather than just a book, you'll find the right buyers, your book will find the right readers, and you'll sell more.

Lisa Pelto, President, Concierge Marketing Publishing Services
ConciergeMarketing.com

Your book's technical specifications:

page count .... **trim size** ....
total of numbered and unnumbered pages   *i.e., 5.5" x 8.5" or 8" x 10"*

binding .... **paper** ....
hardcover, softcover, Smythe sewn, etc.   *i.e., 60# white offset or 60# Cougar Cream opaque*

other details ....
i.e., embossed cover, dust jacket, French Flaps, color or black-and-white interior

....

How many books did you print? Did you use digital, offset, POD, or a combination?

....

....

JOY! Date your book went to press. Was this your original deadline?

....

What was the first thing you did after the book went to press?

....

....

....

....

Date the books arrived: . . . .

How did you feel when you first held a copy of your book?

. . . .

. . . .

. . . .

. . . .

. . . .

. . . .

Did the books look like you expected?

. . . .

. . . .

. . . .

. . . .

Place a photo here of you receiving your new book.

BRAVO!

LET YOUR
LIGHT SHINE

LOVE   JOY   PEACE

PATIENCE   KINDNESS   GOODNESS

FAITHFULNESS GENTLENESS   SELF-CONTROL

Marketing & Publicity

Marketing can be fun or frightening for authors. Getting the word out about your book means spreading your message. Your book can't entertain or inform if nobody knows it's out there. The passion you have for your book can be contagious. Let it show!

Building a launch team was probably my favorite part of self-publishing my first book.

About a month before my children's book was ready for print, I assembled a group made up of parents, grandparents, and teachers in my local community and beyond to rally behind the project. Carefully chosen members of my book's target audience, the launch team gave valuable input and feedback on the book's cover and interior layout design, helped create excitement about the book's pending release through social media, and published reviews of the book on booksellers' websites as soon as it became available for purchase. Facebook provided the ideal avenue both for organizing the launch team and for sharing information about the book with the team's extended network of friends, relatives and co-workers.

The launch culminated in a fun meet-and-greet to celebrate the book's release and thank my team for their continued support and encouragement. Details like a playlist of songs matching the book's theme, gummy "book" worms, and a kids' table with crayons and coloring pages based on illustrations from the book made the launch party a hit with children and adults alike. A friend who is an amateur photographer captured the event, providing beautiful shots for book promotion.

The best thing about the party was connecting one-on-one with those who have believed in my publishing dream and in me as an author from day one. Getting to share that moment with my two young daughters was icing on the cake.

LAUREN FLAKE, author, *Where Did My Sweet Grandma Go?*
LoveofDixie.com

PUBLICITY vs SOCIAL MEDIA
What does your book need?

Many authors come to a literary publicity firm searching for PR help, only to discover they aren't ready for a publicity campaign. That's okay! (Really.) There's a time and a place for everything, and it can be a struggle to identify where and when you should be focusing your book marketing efforts.

Typically, a publicity campaign will include traditional and/or online media outreach — the former focusing on media outreach across print, radio, and TV outlets, while the latter stretches across digital platforms, including blog tours and online news websites. These types of campaigns are standard for authors who are industry experts seeking to further carve out their niche, with an added focus on a long-term impact on their fanbase.

Traditional PR campaigns aren't always well-suited to first-time authors.

However, traditional PR campaigns aren't always well-suited to first-time authors or self-published authors who lack the "meat + bones" to back up their media appeal. That doesn't mean PR outreach isn't for you; it simply means you need to establish your expertise first to make the media more likely to say "yes" to you and your content.

This is where social media comes in, making it an ideal option for those looking to build their platform, gain new readers, and establish a little street credibility. Social media marketing is more than just posting: "buy my book, buy my book, buy my book." It's about building a relationship with your audience that engages them and brings them back for more. Trust us, if you do nothing but sell to your audience, they won't click "buy," they'll click "unfollow."

PR is BETTER FOR...	SM is BETTER FOR...
Established authors	Debut authors
Industry experts (non-fiction authors)	Growing your expertise (and fan base)
Print books	E-book only
Long-term impact	Long-term impact
$$ to $$$	$ to $$

Jandra Sutton, digital marketing director at PR by the Book
PRbytheBook.com

Did you hire a marketing and/or PR firm to help? (Name, company, contact info, date hired)

. . . .

. . . .

. . . .

Marketing plans:

. . . .

. . . .

. . . .

. . . .

. . . .

. . . .

. . . .

. . . .

LAUNCH PARTY
List details such as where, when, who attended, how many books sold, etc.

How did you use social media to promote your book?

....

....

....

....

....

What worked and what didn't?

....

....

....

....

....

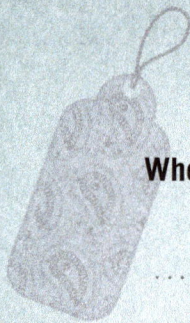

Where is your book being sold? Donated?

....

....

....

....

....

....

....

....

**Did you pursue non-bookstore sales to retailers (discount stores, supermarkets)?
Non-retail buyers (corporations, schools) for bulk sales?**

....

....

....

Did you hire a distributor? (Name, company, contact info, date hired)

....

....

....

What awards competitions did you enter? What awards did you win? Did you attend a ceremony? What does it feel like to be an award-winning author?

....

....

....

....

....

....

....

....

What others are saying now that your book is out. Your favorite reviews or testimonials.

Reaching your dream
is not the
end of the road,
but the beginning of
a new journey.

Reflections

Whew! How are you feeling right now? Some authors are exhausted, some are exhilarated, many a combination of both. Take a moment to look back in wonder at what just happened. Whether it took a few months or several years, your accomplishment is a big deal. Just wait until you discover how your book is going to influence readers and take you places you may have never dreamed.

. . . .

It was all worth it! Writing a book is much like pregnancy and childbirth. As parents, we are filled with so much love for this unborn child, yet there is so much planning and preparation to ensure that the book is ready for its arrival.

I can remember when I was in my final trimester with my first book — an illustrated Christian children's book. The business was ready, I had everything purchased and prepared, and I was eager to "push print." God reminded me that the purpose for this child is ministry.

Each book has its own purpose. It's so easy to get caught up in our to-do list that we lose focus on why we've become an author. Recalling the plan for this baby, this book, and how it would make a difference in the lives of others allowed me to move forward with confidence.

Well, it's been almost a year since I "gave birth" and I'm happy to report that we are doing well! We are working on marketing and have met some great people since we started. I encourage you to enjoy this journey and never lose sight of the purpose and promise of your book.

TERRI L. BELL, author, *I Am Who God Says That I Am*
KingdomKidsBooks.com, KingdomKidsFoundation.org

What are the top three things you learned through the process?

What was the most difficult part of publishing your book?

....

....

....

....

What was the most rewarding?

....

....

....

....

....

....

What went the way you thought it might?

....

....

....

....

....

....

....

....

....

....

....

....

What would you have done differently?

....

....

....

....

....

....

What, if any, road blocks did you encounter along the way?

....

....

....

....

....

Did your book take you somewhere (place, mental state, career) you never thought you'd go? Describe.

Moving Forward

Where do you go from here? This can be the start of a new chapter in your career. Will you forge new relationships with readers, partner with authors on a similar mission, or help others on their first publishing adventure? Will you continue writing? Go on a speaking tour? Remembering that your book is enriching the lives of its readers can fuel your passion as an author, especially if you're a bit weary from the trip.

I wrote *Moving Forward on Your Own: A Financial Guidebook for Widows* after my husband died. The writing process became an important part of my own healing, although I mainly wanted to help my "widowed sisters" who didn't feel confident about money matters. Filled with original paintings and inspirational quotes, the guidebook was designed to help heal a widow's soul as well as her financial issues.

Writing my book was definitely a journey, but what happened after the book was published was even more exciting! That's when my "encore career" as a speaker began. I developed a sponsorship program where others paid me a speaking fee and travel expenses to talk about my work with widows, including the guidebook. A major financial firm asked to co-brand my guidebook, giving it to thousands of their members. I've presented more than 100 sessions in person and in webinars across the country. There are now over 54,000 copies in circulation, and I've published several shorter eBooklets related to my work with widows.

Yes, what began as writing my book expanded far beyond. You might even say that this book redesigned my life, as I've gone from heartbreak to breakthrough and assisted many other widows along the way. I thank God and my guardian angel above for opening the door to a meaningful new life with a rich purpose.

KATHLEEN M. REHL, Ph.D., CFP®, CeFT™, speaker, mentor, and author, *Moving Forward On Your Own*, KathleenRehl.com

YOU ARE MORE THAN JUST A BOOK

Being a successful author isn't about writing the book; it's about living out the reason behind why you decided to write your book in the first place.

As you move forward as an author, it's important to establish a clear vision, while allowing for flexibility and opportunity along the way. After my first book, *Iggy the Iguana*, came out in 2008, it was clear that I had to create my own niche market in order to produce a name for myself and my soon-to-be ten books to follow. Due to a background in professional counseling, I've always had a passion to influence children through stories about acceptance and diversity. My books allowed me to teach students how to develop their own characters and stories. This idea launched a 200-school book tour over the course of five years across Texas and California. Librarians and principals talk, so one recommendation led to the next. Ultimately it had nothing to do with me or my books, but rather the take away that the audience, the students, and teachers, got out of my school visits. That's key as a writer: the most important person in your career is not you – it's your reader. People will see a love for what you do if you are writing for something bigger than yourself. Writing a book for yourself is a journal, no matter the genre. Embracing authorship is about your reader, which is why as authors we should never become too attached to our first rough drafts or even our final copies.

The most important person in your career is not you...

The key is to always listen to what your buyers want next. Listening to my readers (teachers and parents in addition to the kids) led me to make the transition from writing chapter books to picture books. English books were translated into Spanish. I founded the iWRITE literacy organization, which publishes 3rd – 12th graders across the nation and produces an interactive writers' journal for kids. Workshops turned into conferences and later television segments. Each idea or topic fulfilled a need for the audience. Even though I was writing children's fiction, I provided relatable non-fiction advice and techniques. These experiences led me to work with other authors at my small publishing company. After publishing for my clients, I started to consult on how to market, making sure my clients understood their audience when speaking, advertising, and selling. Again reminding authors, it's not about you; it's about your niche, target market.

The opportunities out there for authors are endless if you have a niche. How will you separate yourself from all of the millions of people writing books these days? The authors who succeed found a way to separate themselves and become memorable. Never forget the reason why you wrote your book, because that will be what pushes you past the threshold on days you want to give up. In the words of Christopher Vogler, it's your threshold guardian who asks, "How bad do you really want it?"

Melissa M. Williams, author and founder of iWRITE
MelissaMWilliamsAuthor.com, iWRITE.org

How do you hope others will be impacted because of reading your book?

....

....

....

....

....

....

....

....

....

....

....

....

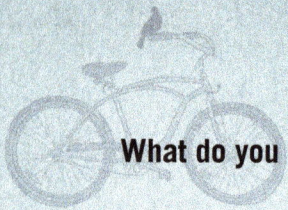

What do you want to do next? What is your focus for the next 12 months?

....

....

....

....

....

....

Is there anything you would change when you write your next book?

....

....

....

....

....

Do you plan to write another book? What will you write? When do you plan to publish it?

....

....

....

....

....

....

....

....

....

....

....

Record stories you've heard from readers who were touched by your book.

About the Authors

Tamara Dever, Erin Stark, and Monica Thomas are the creative force behind TLC Graphics in Austin, Texas. They have been providing award-winning book design, production, and consulting services to independent and small publishers for more than twenty years. Their dedication to helping authors share their passion through publishing is valued across the globe. Along with great design, they share a passion for Jesus, family, and the relationships built with their clients.

TLCGraphics.com

About the Illustrator

Elizabeth Dotterer is a self-taught mixed media artist. She loves working with acrylics and collage elements, and this is her first adventure into the world of publishing. Through her art, she hopes that others smile and feel a sense of the joy and peace that God brings. Elizabeth lives with her husband, her tuxedo cat, and her black Lab in Austin, Texas.

ElizabethDottererArt.com

www.ingramcontent.com/pod-product-compliance
Lightning Source LLC
Chambersburg PA
CBHW040247100426

42811CB00011B/1182